IN SEARCH OF

THE GREAT BEARS

WRITTEN & PHOTOGRAPHED BY BUCK WILDE

*To my father,
whose love of the natural world
inspired me to live with the great bears.*

Written and photographed by Buck Wilde
Designed by Nicola Evans

© 1995 Shortland Publications Inc.

04 03 02 01 00
11 10 9 8 7 6 5

All rights reserved.

Published by Shortland Publications Inc.

Distributed in the United States of America by

a division of Reed Elsevier Inc.
500 Coventry Lane
Crystal Lake, IL 60014
800-822-8661

Printed through Bookbuilders, Hong Kong.

ISBN: 0-7901-0921-2

CONTENTS

CHAPTER ONE:
Grizzly, the Great Bear of North America   4

CHAPTER TWO:
Spring Wake-Up   10

CHAPTER THREE:
Native Americans and the Great Bear   18

CHAPTER FOUR:
A Summer's Fishing   23

CHAPTER FIVE:
Make Way for People!   29

CHAPTER SIX:
Grizzly Autumn   34

CHAPTER SEVEN:
The Last Grizzlies Are Endangered   40

CHAPTER EIGHT:
Winter Nap   42

CHAPTER ONE

Grizzly, the Great Bear of North America

Grizzly bears are descendants of an ancient, nomadic bear that lived in Eurasia several million years ago and crossed the land bridge that connected Alaska and Siberia during the ice ages about 50,000 years ago.

As temperatures rose and the glaciers receded, these bears migrated to the Pacific coast of southern Alaska, where they fished for salmon. Over several millennia, they followed the coastal salmon runs southward to what is now California. Eventually, they followed the wild, free-flowing rivers eastward into the Sierra Nevada mountains and, finally, the northern Rocky Mountains. They lived in diverse habitats, including high deserts, subarctic tundra, temperate grasslands, coastal flats, coniferous forests, and rugged mountains.

Black bears, known for their tree-climbing ability, adapted to life in the forests of North America.

Polar bears adapted to life within the Arctic Circle.

As they moved around, the grizzlies learned how to supplement their diet of fish and wild plants, and occasionally hunted the elk, deer, and bison that inhabited the grassy plains east of the Rockies.

At the height of their population, more than 100,000 grizzly bears inhabited North America between Alaska and Mexico. The bears coexisted in a natural balance of power with two other groups of predators: aboriginal (or native) people and wolves.

While most animal behavior is instinctive, the grizzly survives on learned skills – perhaps more so than any other North American animal. Mother grizzlies spend three to four years teaching their cubs how to hunt and gather food. Younger bears wrestle and play like children. (Perhaps this is why the Yavapai tribe of Arizona and Sonora, Mexico, had a saying: They are like people, except they don't make fire.)

CHAPTER TWO

Spring Wake-Up

Thunder rumbles through the high mountains. A seven-year-old grizzly mother wakes from hibernation in late March and leaves her snow-covered den. Her cub is a year old and weighs nearly 100 pounds.

Last year, the cub learned to obey his mother's commands. It was important to stay close as they traveled through the mountains and valleys gathering food. This year, he should learn which plants and roots to eat, and where to find them.

The mother has lost several hundred pounds of fat and is hungry. She leads the way along a familiar mountain lake, where the young bear spots a raccoon fishing along the shore. To reach the valley where they will forage for food, they must cross a river that flows from the mouth of the lake.

Last year, the cub clung to his mother's back while she swam across the river. This year, he will have to swim across on his own. Together, they plunge into the cold waters and begin to swim. The cub is swept away by swift currents and disappears over a waterfall. The mother watches helplessly and cries out in distress.

Drowning is not uncommon among inexperienced cubs, but this cub is lucky. He makes it to shore farther downstream, and is "adopted" by another grizzly with two cubs of her own.

Tender and nutritious spring grasses are sprouting in the valley. After a month of eating grasses and roots, the mother is gaining weight and is strong enough to chase the elk herd that forages in her meadow. She watches their movements from behind a grassy knoll; but a bull elk, sensing her presence, calls out, reminding the herd to stay on the safe side of the river.

A shift in the wind carries a human scent across the mother bear's sensitive nostrils. She spins on her hind feet to locate the intruder and sees a human form sneaking along the river. Before the man notices her, she disappears into the darkness of the forest. She learned the human scent long ago when her two-year-old brother was shot by a bow hunter. It is time for her to leave the valley and return to the safety of higher ground.

14

15

An old male grizzly has been feeding on western spring beauty and bear root. It is late May, and he hasn't seen another bear since last summer. He prefers to live alone, anyway. An afternoon breeze blows across the lake and carries the scent of a female grizzly.

June is the mating season for the great bears. The mother notices the old male and, after several days of watching one another from a distance, she encourages him to approach. They play together for weeks, and mate before going their separate ways.

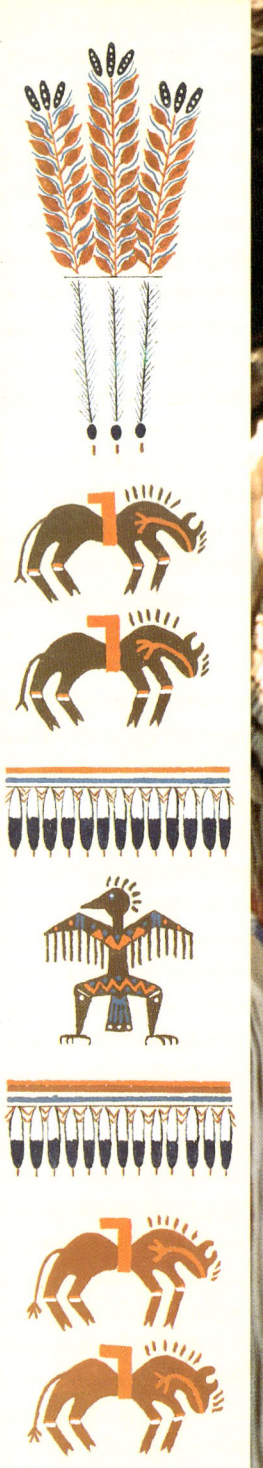

CHAPTER THREE

Native Americans and the Great Bear

Native Americans lived close to the natural world. They rarely took more from the land than they needed, so their needs, and those of the wild animals, were sustained. They traveled the same trails as the grizzly bears, and gathered the same berries, nuts, roots, and seeds. They observed that grizzlies never seemed to get sick and that their wounds healed quickly without infection. They gathered many of the same medicinal herbs that the great bears ate, including yarrow and bear root.

Native Americans respected the great bears as part of the natural world and did not hunt them. The Blackfoot tribes of Montana and Alberta called the grizzly *nitakaio* (the "great bear"). Other tribes in other areas spoke of him with respectful names, such as "Grandmother," "Grandfather," and "Great One."

Native Americans told stories about the animals. The bison showed them virtue. The raven told them stories about how their world was created. The coyote was admired for his cunning. Most powerful of all, however, was the great bear spirit. Even brave warriors whispered when they spoke about the grizzly. They said, "When the needle falls from the pine tree, the eagle sees it, the deer hears it, and the bear smells it."

Sacagawea was a princess of the Shoshoni tribe, who lived in the northern part of the Rocky Mountains. Kidnapped as a young girl, she was later found by the explorers Lewis and Clark.

Sacagawea told her rescuers many stories about the ways of her people. She tried to explain the power of their special animal spirit, the grizzly bear. When the explorers became ill, she treated them with tea made from yarrow. She showed them which berries were safe to eat.

Eventually, she led them to her homeland. The Shoshoni tried to explain that the grizzlies were smart, like people. But the exploration party feared the great bears. They gave the grizzly bear a Latin name, *Ursus arctos horribilis*, and shot many of them. Increasingly, more explorers arrived – and with them, rifles. This marked the beginning of the end for the great bears.

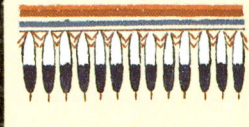

CHAPTER FOUR

A Summer's Fishing

Wildflowers are in bloom. Two four-year-old grizzlies are napping under the shade of some thick bushes. Solstice is blond, with long, shaggy hair. Her brother, Chocolate, has a dark brown coat. No longer cubs, but not yet adults, they are adolescents.

Last year, the cubs shared their mother's salmon catches, but this year they will have to feed themselves. Their mother was killed by a poacher's rifle. If they do not learn to feed themselves well this summer, they will not build up enough fat to survive the coming winter months.

Solstice and Chocolate wake from their nap. Eagles are soaring overhead. This is the signal for which the bears have been waiting. They follow a well-worn trail down toward the river.

   Hungry bears are already waiting in their favorite fishing spots along the river. Solstice and Chocolate sneak by the adult bears to an unoccupied stretch of river. Solstice jumps into a deep pool below the falls but comes up without a salmon. After a second try, she's got one! She sits down in the cool water and eats her catch. Soon she has a second one.

   Chocolate isn't so skilled. Regardless of all his splashing around, the spawning salmon swim by him untouched. After eating her third fish, Solstice catches another and tosses it to Chocolate. Unashamed, he eats.

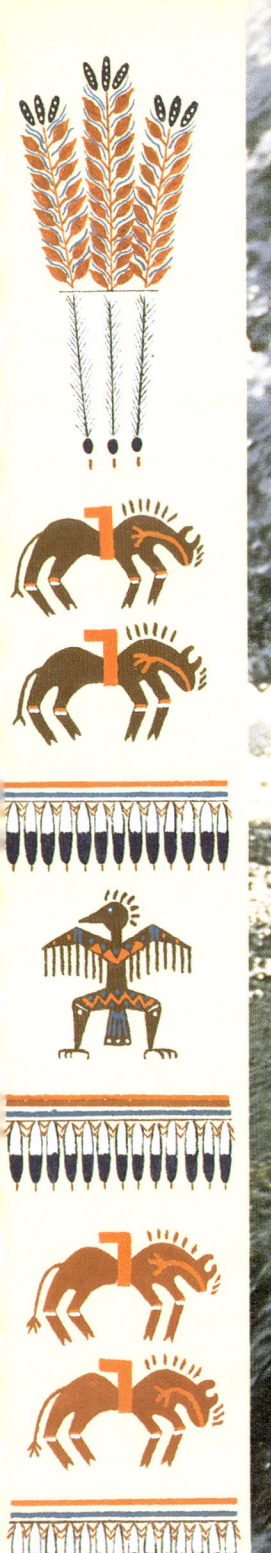

The next day, Solstice and Chocolate are chased out of the estuary by a fishing boat. The fishermen lay a net across the width of the river, and are soon pulling salmon into the boat. The fishermen stay for a week, catching the fish as they enter the river. The bears finally leave, hungry and frustrated.

If they are going to survive, the young bears must find another stream where the salmon are running. Until then, they will have to find other things to eat.

CHAPTER FIVE

Make Way for People!

The grizzly's cousin, the European brown bear, inhabited much of Europe, and early astronomers named two constellations, *Ursa Major* (the Big Bear) and *Ursa Minor* (the Little Bear), in their honor.

The North American bears, therefore, did not come as a surprise to early European explorers on the Pacific coast. Ranchers, trappers, and miners followed the explorers and shot thousands of the great bears as they cleared their new land, believing they were making it safer for their cattle and settlements.

In the Midwest, Native American tribes and blond grizzlies relied for part of their diet on the massive ungulate herds of antelope, bison, elk, and deer of the Great Plains.

As the U.S. Government claimed more territories after the Civil War, it paid bounty hunters to slaughter bison to make way for the new landowners. The settlers themselves shot vast numbers of other ungulates, and thousands of the Great Plains grizzlies. The bears' grasslands were fenced off and plowed under. By the end of the nineteenth century, blond grizzlies were extinct.

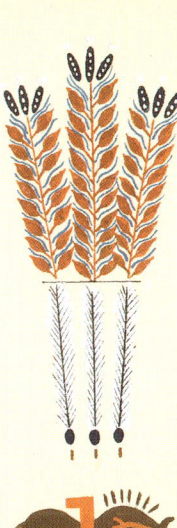

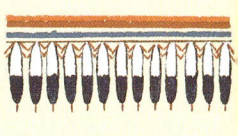

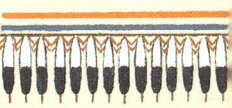

31

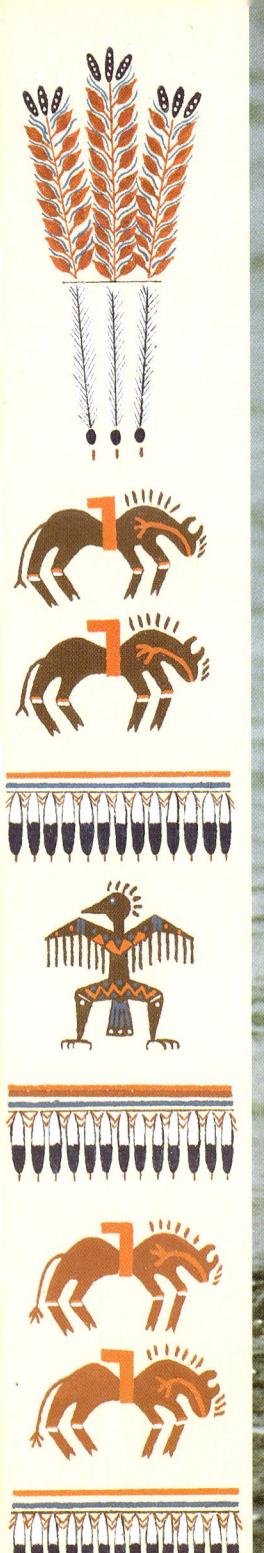

The Rocky Mountains offered the grizzly bear a last hiding place from human rifles. However, over the last century, mining, logging, ranching, and increased settlement interfered with this last wild habitat.

Before hydroelectric dams interrupted the wild flow of many rivers, salmon provided a dependable food supply. Today, the salmon species of the northern Rockies are themselves endangered, and populations are down along the great spawning rivers of the Pacific.

CHAPTER SIX

Grizzly Autumn

Silvertip is twelve years old and in the prime of her life. She has no cubs, but has carried three fertilized eggs inside of her since mid-June. They will not begin to develop until later this fall, shortly after she goes to her den to hibernate for the winter.

She is able to fish and gather berries over the summer months, and to store as much fat as possible, instead of using up all her energy nurturing the developing babies.

It is early September, and the first frost has appeared. Leaves are turning yellow and red, and berries are falling to the ground. The ptarmigan has begun to change from brown to white, indicating winter is on its way. Silvertip's keen nose picks up the scent of a patch of berries that escaped last night's frost. She gorges herself for two hours without lifting her head.

With her enormous appetite temporarily satisfied, she lumbers down to the river and drinks. She looks over both shoulders and sniffs the autumn air. She smells a bull moose, who is watching her from the safety of his thicket.

On the opposite side of the valley, the elk are rutting. Silvertip can smell and hear them. An old bull, tired from defending the herd, would make easy prey! She fords the river and heads into the wind.

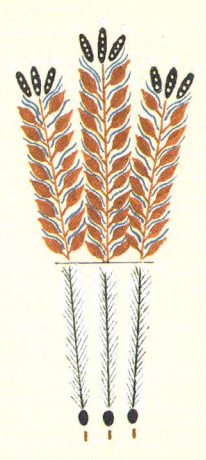

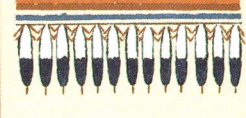

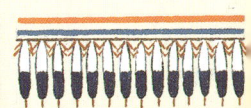

38

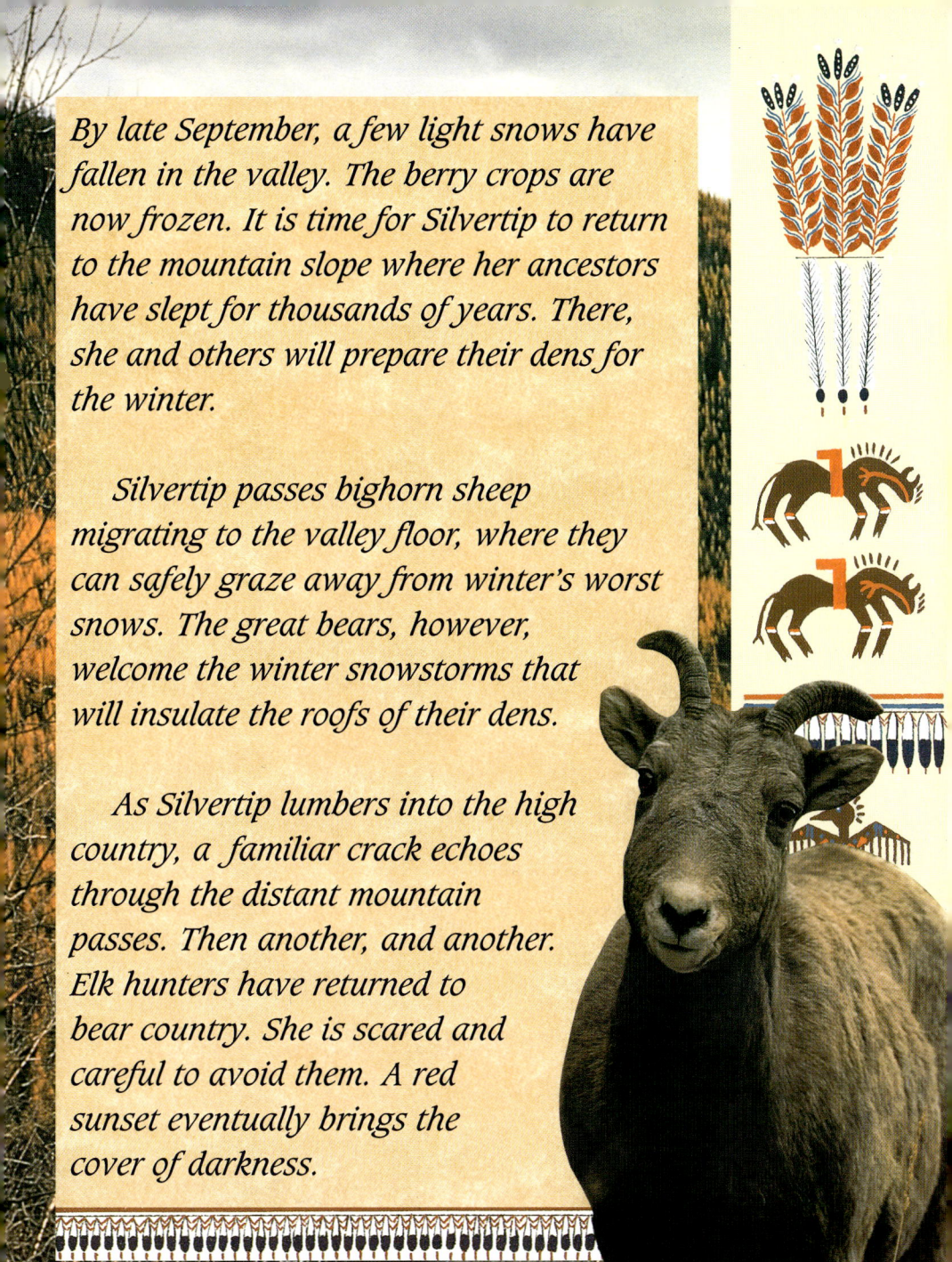

By late September, a few light snows have fallen in the valley. The berry crops are now frozen. It is time for Silvertip to return to the mountain slope where her ancestors have slept for thousands of years. There, she and others will prepare their dens for the winter.

Silvertip passes bighorn sheep migrating to the valley floor, where they can safely graze away from winter's worst snows. The great bears, however, welcome the winter snowstorms that will insulate the roofs of their dens.

As Silvertip lumbers into the high country, a familiar crack echoes through the distant mountain passes. Then another, and another. Elk hunters have returned to bear country. She is scared and careful to avoid them. A red sunset eventually brings the cover of darkness.

CHAPTER SEVEN
The Last Grizzlies Are Endangered

According to the biological study of population dynamics, once a grizzly population falls to between 50-90 bears, it will quickly become extinct. Birthrates among grizzlies are very low. The females produce on average only two cubs, and give birth once every three years.

This is why there is great concern for the only two populations of grizzly bears remaining in the United States. There are fewer than 400 bears in each group, and their locations are far apart. Both of these groups are threatened by habitat destruction and human encroachment.

Government agencies are working to better manage the great bears' wilderness areas, in the hope that this will allow their populations to recover. But grizzly numbers continue to decline; and some biologists fear that one, or both, of these populations is headed for extinction. The answer may be a proposal to introduce a third group of bears between the two existing populations. This would open a corridor for the bears, and perhaps assure their survival.

WHAT CAN WE DO?

1. Observe bear safety rules when visiting bear country.

2. Support worldwide efforts to protect endangered species.

REWARD

NATIONAL AUDUBON SOCIETY will pay up to **$15,000** for **INFORMATION** leading to the arrest and conviction of anyone **ILLEGALLY KILLING** a **GRIZZLY BEAR** or transporting grizzly bear hides or parts

CONTACT
U.S. Fish and Wildlife Service

CHAPTER EIGHT

Winter Nap

Grandfather is old and wise. He has escaped bullets, baited traps, and tranquilizer darts in his 24 years. Shifting November winds tell him that a large snowstorm is coming to the high country soon. He has always hibernated on this same remote mountainside, far from roads or hiking trails that would invite humans.

The sun is low in the afternoon sky as Grandfather ambles down to the mountain lake for a last drink. His coat is covered with frost. He drinks until his belly is full. Click, click, click. A familiar sound travels across the lake. He looks into the camera. Click, click again. The photographer stands and folds his tripod. Grandfather is unconcerned and walks away from the lake toward his den. The photographer walks in the opposite direction with the tripod over his shoulder.

43

A storm blows across the mountain as Grandfather falls asleep, confident that his tracks have been covered by the falling snow. Over the cold winter months, he will rustle in his deep sleep, but will not wake to eat or drink. The great bear's miraculous metabolism will convert the hundreds of pounds of fat into heat to warm him without producing body wastes.

   Winter's snows will insulate his den entrance and ensure his survival until longer and warmer spring days wake him. He sleeps unaware that the mechanical rumble he heard earlier was from the construction of a logging road. Next spring, bulldozers, dynamite, helicopters, and chain saws will drive him to another wild hiding place – if one can be found!

45

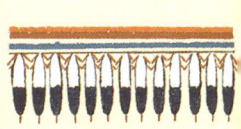

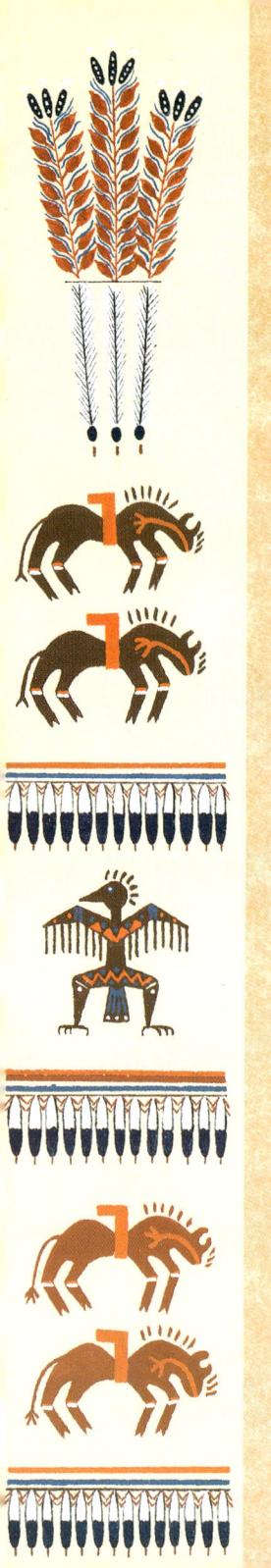

GLOSSARY

behavior:
    learned – a pattern of behavior which an animal has to learn
    instinctive – a pattern of behavior with which an animal is born
bounty hunter – a person who hunts animals for money
constellation – a cluster of fixed stars that has an outline which resembles a figure
estuary – a wide, tidal river mouth
extinct – describes a species that has died out
forage – to search for food
habitat – an area in which an animal or plant lives
hibernation – an inactive state in which an animal's metabolism slows down in order to survive the cold and lack of food in winter
hydroelectric dam – a structure that captures, stores, and controls the force of moving water to generate electricity
knoll – a small hill
metabolism – the process of converting food into energy that occurs in living organisms
migration – the movement of animals from one place to another, usually a seasonal move for food and warmth
millennium – a period of 1,000 years
Native Americans – the indigenous people of North America
nutritious – food that contains nourishment
poacher – a person who catches animals illegally
ptarmigan – a bird whose appearance changes from black or gray plumage in summer to white in the winter
rutting – mating activity among animals such as deer
spawning – describes aquatic animals, such as salmon, that produce large numbers of eggs
thicket – a dense growth of small trees
ungulate – a group of animals that have hooves

TITLES IN THE SERIES

SET 9A

Television Drama
Time for Sale
The Shady Deal
The Loch Ness Monster Mystery
Secrets of the Desert

SET 9B

To JJ From CC
Pandora's Box
The Birthday Disaster
The Song of the Mantis
Helping the Hoiho

SET 9C

Glumly
Rupert and the Griffin
The Tree, the Trunk, and the Tuba
Errol the Peril
Cassidy's Magic

SET 9D

Barney
Get a Grip, Pip!
Casey's Case
Dear Future
Strange Meetings

SET 10A

A Battle of Words
The Rainbow Solution
Fortune's Friend
Eureka
It's a Frog's Life

SET 10B

The Cat Burglar of Pethaven Drive
The Matchbox
In Search of the Great Bears
Many Happy Returns
Spider Relatives

SET 10C

Horrible Hank
Brian's Brilliant Career
Fernitickles
It's All in Your Mind,
　James Robert
Wing High, Gooftah

SET 10D

The Week of the Jellyhoppers
Timothy Whuffenpuffen-
　Whippersnapper
Timedetectors
Ryan's Dog Ringo
The Secret of Kiribu Tapu Lagoon